Little Star

By

Deborah Jean Solberg

Illustrations

by

Joseph G. Bakos

Little Star
2nd Edition 2025
Copyright © 2015 by Deborah J. Solberg
All rights reserved. No part of this book may be reproduced or transmitted in any form or by any means without written permission of the author.
ISBN: **978-1-990442-10-0**
A SUNCITY PRODUCTIONS BOOK FOR CHILDREN
Contemporary fairy-tale with the magic of a spiritual wand.
For more information, visit the website:
DeborahJeanSolberg.com

Little Star was the newest baby star.
He lived with Father Sun and Mother Moon in the
constellations circling Planet Earth.

Little Star had a lot to learn about being a real star.

Father Sun and Mother Moon told Little Star,
*"Watch carefully, son.
Soon, you will know when to shine your light."*

Little Star looked down on Earth, a pretty planet of blue and green.

'What a strange world down there.
So many little humans,
in different sizes and shapes and colors,
all bumping around and into each other on land, sea and air.
It is better to be high in the sky, with the rest of the stars.'

One day, Little Star heard crying.
Down from the sky, he saw children yell and laugh
at a little girl named Debbie.

She tried to stop the girls from throwing sand in the sandbox
and the boys from stomping on her sandcastle.

But it was too late.
   The sandcastle was flat.
      Sand was everywhere, even her hair.
         Her tears washed sand out of her eyes.

The children told Debbie it was her fault and ran away.
   All the castles in her sandbox were broken.

      "Mommy, daddy...look down the   re.
         That little girl is crying.
            What should we do?'

Mother Moon said,
   "Little Star. That happens all the time on Earth.
      We can't fix all those sandboxes,
         or all those people.
            They are on Planet Earth
            to learn how to get along."

Little Star was sad.
   "But they want her to cry and then laugh at her.

Mother Moon and Father Sun didn't talk out loud.
   They read each other's minds.

They thought it was time for Little Star to learn
   why there are stars.

Father Sun said,

"Little Star, you are right.
What you see, needs to be changed.
But we must have permission to help a human.
When Debbie looks up at the moon and the stars,
she might ask for help.

Then trust yourself to do the right thing.'

Sure enough, when Father Sun said goodnight,
and Mother Moon rose high in the sky,
Little Star saw Debbie sit in her broken sandbox
and look up in wonder.

"Everything is gone...
my sandcastle, the sandbox.
Everyone who was my friend.
All gone.
I don't want to play anymore."

The STARS sparkled as though to say,
"We are here. We are your friends.
We'll never leave you. We'll never hurt you."

Little Star was puzzled.
"But she can't hear us.
Mama, aren't we going to say something to her that she can hear?"

Mother Moon said,
"When humans cry, they hear only their own sadness.
We will shine light on her, so she knows she's not alone."

"But I want to do something,"

Little Star waved his points.

"You are doing something, Little Star.
You are here where she can see you,
so, twinkle your very best,
and she will look at you the most.
Then she will know you are a friend."
Said Mother Moon.

Little Star thought about that.

He looked around to see how the other stars twinkled.

He asked North Star,
"How do you twinkle, North Star?"

North Star chuckled.
"I don't twinkle.
I'm the North Star.
I shine the brightest
so everyone knows where to find me and don't get lost."

Then, he asked Big Dipper and Little Dipper.
"How do you twinkle?"

Big Dipper said,

> *"We don't really have to twinkle
> because everyone recognizes us by our shape."*

Little Dipper laughed,

> *"Yeah. We look like dippers!"*

Debbie would never look at him next to all these famous stars.

So Little Star waved at Orion.
"How do you twinkle, Orion?"

Orion said,
"I am a 'we', and 'we' are not a star.
We're a constellation."

Each star around Orion echoed the other.

Little Star knew he couldn't compete with a group of stars.

Little Star stared at Milky Way and wondered how many stars it took to look like a swirling snowstorm.

Milky Way didn't really twinkle either. It glowed!

Little Star felt very small.

He saw sand slip though Debbie's sad fingers.

He wanted her to look up at him.

Not the North Star, or the Dippers or Orion or Milky Way. Only, him.

He wanted her to smile.

Little Star polished his points and imagined the energy of Mother Moon and Father Sun swirl inside him.

Then, he imagined shooting that energy out of his five points stronger than the moonbeams or sunlight.

He peeked down to see if Debbie was looking up.

And she was!

She looked up like she was searching for something.

He was so happy, that he started to hum a little tune.

His light began to dance.

And then, it happened.

Debbie's head turned in his direction and stared right at him!

He was overjoyed and he danced a little bit more.
Little Star twinkled ... just for her.

Debbie smiled.

Her head tilted side to side, as though she was dancing with him.

He was so excited.
He didn't notice the other stars turn to look at him.
He didn't see his mother's pride.
All he saw was Debbie, who now looked happy.

She got out of the sandbox and brushed the sand off her clothes.

Looking up at Little Star, she did a happy dance and giggled.

Little Star did a happy dance and giggled.

Then they just stared at each other
        like there was no one else anywhere else.

Finally, Debbie waved goodnight
        and went to her room to sleep.

But she couldn't sleep.
All she could think about was the next day,
when the children who ruined her sandbox
would return.

It was a game to them,
a fun thing to destroy her sandbox and make her cry.
It made them smile inside,
as they yelled and threw things.

There were so many of them and only one of her.

*"What happens tomorrow, mama,
when those children come and kick sand?
Debbie won't be able to see me then, and she'll cry again."*

Mother Moon said,

*"Your father will be there to remind her it's a new day,
and every new day means a chance to change."*

Little Star wasn't sure.

"But Debbie *can't change them."*

His mother agreed.

*"No, she can't. But what do you think she can change?
What did you change so you could help her?"*

Little Star thought for a minute.

*"Me!
But how can she change herself?
Aren't they still going to be mean and make her sad?'*

Mother Moon smiled.

*"Let's watch what happens while she sleeps.
I will shine light in Debbie's mind
so she believes she can change
how she reacts to them."*

Mother Moon painted pictures in Debbie's mind
that she would understand.

Debbie dreamed of a cross that beamed light
like the moon and sun together.

It became like a tree inside her and made her feel strong.

She felt like its branches lift her off the ground.

But she was afraid.

She felt the energies of the children coming to attack her again.

Suddenly on top of the cross inside her,
     there appeared a revolving eye – just like a lighthouse lamp.

Her mind said,
          'Do not fear. The eye will see them coming.'

Then she heard in her dream,
     'Before they can hurt you again, we will give you a third gift.'

Little Star asked his mother,

> *"Is this what we do when people look up?*
> *Give them answers to questions?"*

Mother Moon nodded,

> *"Yes, son. We light the way.*
> *We give hope because when everything is dark,*
> *light is magical."*

That made Little Star feel light and bright and he twinkled again.

He was excited that his job was to help others.

Mother Moon said,

> *"Now son, watch this.*
> Debbie *is going to get the most important gift of all."*

In her dream, Debbie saw the third gift.

It flipped like a comic book.

Father Sun painted the most exciting picture of all.

Above the revolving eye, a new STAR exploded.

The new STAR had points in many different directions,
with rainbow-colored music all playing together.

And, just in time!

The revolving eye locked onto the energy of the bullies
and sent it to the new STAR.

The new STAR inhaled the bully's energy, and blew up,
spreading pure white light in the universe.

All the STARS waited to see what Debbie would do next.

When Debbie woke up, she knew that
the bullies would be at the sandbox to make her cry.

But she didn't feel like the same person she was yesterday.

She couldn't see the stars, but she knew they were there.

Father Sun smiled down on her, and she smiled back.

She remembered her dream. It gave her an idea for a sandcastle.

She thought about looking for a new sandbox,
        but she didn't think that was the answer to the problem.

No...she would go back to her sandbox.
Building sandcastles was like breathing air.
It was all she ever wanted to do.

She made a plan in her mind.
She would invite them to build a sandcastle.

Make one, instead of break one.

She smiled a thank you to the stars,
 for helping her mind to make the pictures, and a
 special thank you to Little Star.

'You made me want to dance again".

Little Star could hear her thoughts and see the pictures in her mind.

'Thoughts are very powerful'.
He thought.   The rest of the STARS twinkled in agreement.

*"Human beings don't know how powerful they are.
If they did, they would think nicer thoughts."*

Little Star was amazed that invisible thoughts were so powerful.

*"Little Star...thoughts are the beginning of creating something.
Imagination is like a big paintbrush that sweeps color into action,
and then we see a painting."*

Little Star said,
 "I can hardly wait to see Debbie's new sandcastle."

Mother Moon said,
 *"Yes, it will be even better than before because of what happened.
She will build that into the sandcastle.
It is always better when everyone works together."*

Little Star sighed,
> *"I wish I could build a sandcastle in a sandbox."*

> *"You do already, Little Star.*
> *You just build it in a different way.*
> *The humans on earth are our sandbox."*
> *"and Debbie was your sandcastle."*

Father Sun and Mother Moon said,

> *"Now I get it. Wow!"*

Litle Star was so happy.

Mother Moon and Father Sun were very proud of their Little Star.

He made a beautiful sandcastle
        by making a difference in someone's life.
            He made it better.

LIttle Star knew he had done one of the most important things
        he would ever do.
            He helped someone be happy.

And happiness makes everyone shine!

The End

About the Author

Deborah Jean Solberg

Is founding Artistic Director of Theatrix Youtheatre Society located in British Columbia, Canada. Theatrix was incorporated as a non-profit charitable performing arts organization for children in 1991. Over the last three decades, she collaborated with thousands of children to create shows as a vehicle to learn confidence and self-expression.

Deborah produced and directed over 100 productions, from short school touring shows to full scale musical theatre productions and is a 17-time Theatre BC festival award winner.

Deborah is playwright of over 30 original plays, with a passion for adapting classical children's literature.   Deborah's own children's stories have a strong spiritual context to help shape the character of children into kind and compassionate human beings. Each story has been inspired by real people or real events.

Deborah has not only had the pleasure of watching several alumni become professional actors, dancers. and singers around the world but is proud of the many friendships that have endured over time.

She hopes her readership enjoys her take on the contemporary fairy tale.

About the Illustrator

Joseph G. Bakos

Joseph worked for Varga Cartoon Studios, which worked on Rugrats, Mr. Bean Cartoons, Real Monsters, etc.

He has also worked in game developing for more than 10 years. at Invictus Games Ltd.

Joseph continues to work freelance on children's books, comics, web design and other illustrations.

****

Other Children's Books in the
Empowerment Stories Series
by
Deborah Jean Solberg

The Happy Mirror
Rain Dancer
My Favorite
Super Cape
The Golden Rule

Check out DeborahJeanSolberg.com
https://www.facebook.com/deborahjeansolberg

(Please report any book quality issues.)

www.ingramcontent.com/pod-product-compliance
Lightning Source LLC
Chambersburg PA
CBHW042138030726
47599CB00002B/520